From Here To Eternity:
A SURVIVAL GUIDE

WillieG

WestBow
PRESS
A DIVISION OF THOMAS NELSON

Additional copies of this book in various formats may be ordered through www.ChristianSelfPublishers.com

Scripture quotations marked NLT are taken from the Holy Bible, New Living Translation, copyright 1996, 2004. Used by permission of Tyndale House Publishers, Inc., Wheaton, Illinois 60189. All rights reserved.

WestBow Press books may be ordered through booksellers or by contacting:

WestBow Press
A Division of Thomas Nelson
1663 Liberty Drive
Bloomington, IN 47403
www.westbowpress.com
1-(866) 928-1240

ISBN: 978-1-4497-1654-7 (sc)
ISBN: 978-1-4497-1655-4 (e)

Library of Congress Control Number: 2011928156

Printed in the United States of America

WestBow Press rev. date: 06/08/2011

1

From Here To Eternity

Most likely, you are reading this because:

a) Christians have vanished in numbers and you are trying to understand what happened.

b) Christians have not suddenly vanished in spite of the fact that it seems to you that "The Tribulation" spoken of in the Bible has already begun.

c) You want to examine this material to determine if you should leave a copy on your living room table for those who come looking for you, when you and others who believe as you do, suddenly vanish.

If you are in groups a or b, do not lose heart! You can recover from the situation. Whatever you do, don't abandon your faith in Christ; no matter what! Read on!

Let's start with some working definitions.

Jesus, speaking of a future time in human history, said:

> **(21) For there will be <u>greater anguish</u> than at any time since the world began. And it will never be so great again.**
>
> **(22) In fact, unless that time of calamity is shortened, not a single person will survive. But it will be shortened for the sake of God's chosen ones.**
>
> **MATTHEW 24:21-22 NLT**

The expression ***greater anguish***, in the original Greek text, is the expression ***megas thlipsis***. ***Megas*** means exceedingly great and ***thlipsis*** means anguish or tribulation.

Jesus is referring to a unique period in human history during which the agony-troubles-distress-anguish-tribulation of human earthlings is greater than it ever has been before or ever will be again. Hence, this unique period has become known as **The Great Tribulation**.

The next verse tells us that the events which occur during The Great Tribulation bring mankind to the brink of annihilation. Reread verse 22; stop and think about it! It tells us that God will intervene in human affairs to keep that from happening. It further tells us that He does this because He does not want Christians to suffer through the horror of such an event. Clearly, such a time is still in the future and some number of Christians are still alive at the end of The Great Tribulation or God would not have had to shorten it.

It is very important to understand that many Christians will experience The Great Tribulation. Let me say that again; MANY CHRISTIANS WILL EXPERIENCE THE GREAT TRIBULATION! In his renowned revelation, John speaks of seeing <u>countless</u> Christians from all over the world who experienced The Great Tribulation.

> **(9) After these things I saw, and lo, <u>a great multitude, which to number no one was able, out of all nations, and tribes, and peoples, and tongues, standing before the throne, and before the Lamb, arrayed in white robes,</u> and palms in their hands,**
>
> **(10) and crying with a great voice, saying, 'The salvation *is* to Him who is sitting upon the throne--to our God, and to the Lamb!'**
>
> **(11) And all the messengers stood around the throne, and the elders and the four living creatures, and they fell upon their face, and bowed before God,**
>
> **(12) saying, 'Amen! the blessing, and the glory, and the wisdom, and the thanksgiving, and the honour, and the power, and the strength, *are* to our God-- to the ages of the ages! Amen!'**
>
> **(13) And answer did one of the elders, saying to me, 'These, who have been arrayed with the white robes--who are they, and whence came they?'**
>
> **(14) and I have said to him, 'Sir, thou hast known;' and he said to me, <u>'These are those who are coming out of the great tribulation, and they did wash their robes, and they made their robes white in the blood of the Lamb;</u>**
>
> **(15) because of this are they before the throne of God, and they do service to Him day and night in His sanctuary, and He who is sitting upon the throne shall tabernacle over them;**
>
> **(16) they shall not hunger any more, nor may the sun fall upon them, nor any heat,**
>
> **(17) because the Lamb that *is* in the midst of the throne shall feed them, and shall lead them unto living fountains of waters, and wipe away shall God every tear from their eyes.'**
>
> **REVELATION 7:9-17 YLT**

If you are a Christian and you have found yourself in "The Great Tribulation"; take heart, shout halleluiah! You are in good company!

So, ***The Great Tribulation is that unique period of time when the earth and earthlings experience stress, distress, troubles, agony, and anguish like never before or after.***

It is common to refer to the seven years leading up to the return of Christ as the "The Tribulation" and to refer to the last half of that period as "The Great Tribulation".

Another event related to The Tribulation is "the rapture": In a letter to the church at Thessalonica, Paul speaks of believers being "caught up" into the clouds to meet Jesus when He returns.

> **(13) And now, dear brothers and sisters, we want you to know what will happen to the believers who have died so you will not grieve like people who have no hope.**
>
> **(14) For since we believe that Jesus died and was raised to life again, we also believe that when Jesus returns, God will bring back with Him the believers who have died.**
>
> **(15) We tell you this directly from the Lord: We who are still living <u>when the Lord returns</u> will not meet Him ahead of those who have died.**
>
> **(16) For the Lord Himself will come down from heaven with a commanding shout, with the voice of the archangel, and with the trumpet call of God. First, <u>the Christians who have died will rise from their graves.</u>**
>
> **<u>(17) Then, together with them, we who are still alive and remain on the earth will be caught up in the clouds to meet the Lord in the air</u>. Then we will be with the Lord forever.**
>
> **(18) So encourage each other with these words.**
>
> **(1 Thessalonians 4:13-18 NLT)**

The expression **caught up** in verse 17, is the Greek word **harpazo'** which means to seize, catch away, catch up, pluck or pull away. When this was translated into Latin the Latin verb **raptio**, from which we derive the English word **rapture**, was used. Hence, this act of God, catching up Christians, is simply referred to as "the rapture". Further, those who are not caught up to be with Jesus during this event are referred to as "the left behind".

Above, in 4:13-18, Paul tells us that:

a) Jesus will return.

b) When Jesus returns, He will bring all Christians with Him.

c) Jesus will give a commanding shout.

d) The trumpet call of God will sound.

e) Those Christians who have died will be raised from the dead.

f) Those Christians, who are alive, along with the believers just raised from the dead, will be "raptured" or plucked off the earth by God to be with Jesus at His return.

g) All these believers will ascend together to meet Christ in the air.

h) They will all remain with Christ forever.

Paul also counseled the church at Corinth with these words:

> **(51) But let me reveal to you a wonderful secret. <u>We will not all die, but we will all be transformed!</u>**
>
> **(52) It will happen in a moment, in the blink of an eye, when the last trumpet is blown. For when the trumpet sounds, those who have died will be raised to live forever. And we who are living will also be transformed.**
>
> **(53) For our dying bodies must be <u>transformed into bodies that will never die</u>; our mortal bodies must be transformed into immortal bodies.**
>
> **(54) Then, when our dying bodies have been transformed into bodies that will never die [*and our mortal bodies have been transformed into immortal bodies*], this Scripture will be fulfilled: "Death is swallowed up in victory.**
>
> **(1 Corinthians 15:51-54 NLT)**

In these verses Paul adds that before the believers are raptured, they are transformed into immortal beings with new bodies (verse 54).

So, *"the rapture" is when all Christians, living and dead, are transformed into immortal beings with bodies and plucked from the earth by God to meet Christ in the air.*

OK!

So, where's the problem?

Well:

1. If you <u>are</u> a Christian

   and

   you have always believed in a "pre-tribulation" rapture or a "mid-tribulation" rapture or a "pre-wrath" rapture or such

   and

   you find yourself <u>past that point</u> in The Tribulation

   and the rapture has not occurred

   then you have a problem!

   You need to verify that you, in fact, are in The Tribulation and

   that the rapture has not taken place.

If you can verify that you <u>are</u> in The Tribulation and the rapture <u>has not</u> occurred then you obviously hold a false belief regarding the timing of the rapture. So, you need to jettison your false beliefs and go on. But, be careful! Don't jettison valuable cargo. You need to get prepared to endure more of The Tribulation and to replace your old beliefs with new ones. So, cinch up your belt and read on!

2. If you are a Christian

    and

    you are in The Tribulation

    and

    the rapture <u>has</u> occurred

    then

    you have a serious problem!

    You need to verify

    that you, in fact, are in The Tribulation and

    that the rapture has, in fact, taken place.

If you can verify that you have experienced The Tribulation and that the rapture <u>has</u> occurred then what you thought was Christianity, was insufficient to get you raptured. You are going to have to reevaluate everything you believe about Christianity. Be careful! <u>Don't abandon Christianity now</u>. All you need to do is correct some misunderstandings and then you can join your brothers and sisters who were raptured.

Also, you will need a survival strategy; so keep reading.

3. If you <u>are not</u> a Christian

    but

    you think you may be in The Tribulation

    and

    great numbers of Christians have been raptured

    then

    you have a very big problem!

However, if you now think that:

- Christianity really might be "the way".

- The Bible may really speak true after all.

then I've got good news for you. You can join those that were raptured; so, read on. In fact, even if you don't now believe such things; read on anyway. It can't hurt! You might be wrong and the bottom line is that the consequences are just too dire to risk being wrong.

2

Christian?

John tells of a conversation Jesus had with Nicodemus, one of the Jewish spiritual leaders of His time. He says:

> **(3) Jesus replied, "I tell you the truth, unless you are <u>born again</u>, you cannot see the <u>Kingdom of God</u>."**
>
> **(4) "What do You mean?" exclaimed Nicodemus. "How can an old man go back into his mother's womb and be born again?"**
>
> **(5) Jesus replied, "I assure you, <u>no one can enter the Kingdom of God without being born of water and the Spirit</u>.**
>
> **(6) Humans can reproduce only human life, but the Holy Spirit gives birth to spiritual life.**
>
> **(7) So don't be surprised when I say, 'You must be born again.'**
>
> **(8) The wind blows wherever it wants. Just as you can hear the wind but can't tell where it comes from or where it is going, so you can't explain how <u>people are born of the Spirit</u>."**
>
> JOHN 3:3-8 NLT

The human fetus develops inside a sack of fluid. That sac breaks and the fluid flows out just prior to delivery. Hence, the common expressions, "breaking your water" and "when my water breaks" which are used to communicate that the moment of birth has arrived. When Jesus says we are born of water He is simply saying that we are all physically born into this physical world. But, in contrast, He says there is another birth process we can then go through which brings us spiritually into a spiritual world. A Christian has been physically born and then spiritually born or "born again". When a person is spiritually born, the Holy Spirit of God comes and cohabits their body and communicates with them one-on-one.

> **Don't you realize that your body is the temple of the Holy Spirit, who lives in you and was given to you by God? You do not belong to yourself….**
>
> 1 CORINTHIANS 6:19 NLT

Being "born again" is also referred to as being saved and as being in the Kingdom of God. That's why in John 3:5 above, Jesus said: …"I assure you, no one can enter the Kingdom of God without being born of water and the Spirit."

Note that Jesus ties being born again to being a citizen in the Kingdom of God. God has made Jesus the king over the Kingdom of God.

In his letter to the church in Rome, Paul says:

> **If you confess with your mouth that Jesus is Lord and believe in your heart that God raised Him from the dead, you will be saved.**
>
> ROMANS 10:9 NLT

So, if you commit to serve Jesus as your king and truly believe that God raised Him from the dead and you openly say so; then at that moment you will be born again and the Holy Spirit of God will come and be with you and communicate one-on-one with you. This is why the Bible says:

> **Therefore if any man *be* in Christ, *he is* a new creature: old things are passed away; behold, all things are become new.**
>
> 2 CORINTHIANS 5:17 KJV

Note that the Bible says that once we are "born again" we no longer belong to ourselves. That's because we belong to our king. It is vitally important that you recognize and honor Jesus as your king and literally make Him your Lord and master. Otherwise your "confession" will be empty words. When you mean it and then say it, you will be taken into His kingdom. Know this, if you truly mean it, then you will serve Him 24-7 and do exactly what He tells you to do.

You do not, at that point, receive a new immortal body with new capabilities to think and feel. So, until you listen to the voice of the Holy Spirit speaking to you and follow His instructions, your old habits will prevail. God does not force you to change! But, He does give you the where-with-all to change. When you are born again you can start all over and develop along spiritual lines in accord with God's will and displace your old behavior patterns. **There is no particular level you must achieve in this life**: The key is that you give it all you've got for the rest of your life. If you are prepared to do that, then pray this prayer: "Father God, I come to You to be born again. I openly declare that Jesus is my Lord. I believe that Jesus is Your Son and that He came to Earth to save me from destruction in Satan's dark kingdom and to be a member of Your family in Your kingdom. I declare that He died and that You raised Him from the dead. I ask You to forgive me for everything I have ever done which offended You. From this time forward,

I commit myself to learning and following Your will. Thank You Father and Thank You Jesus for making this possible for me!"

If you earnestly prayed that prayer then you were spiritually "born again" and the Holy Spirit of God has come to cohabit your body with your spirit. But, He does not, so to speak, "fill" you completely up with His Spirit. The Bible tells us that Jesus was the only human whom God completely filled with His Holy Spirit without limit.

> **For He is sent by God. He speaks God's words, for God gives Him the Spirit without limit.**
>
> **JOHN 3:34 NLT**

However, the Bible also tells us:

> **And be not drunk with wine, wherein is excess; but be filled with the Spirit;**
>
> **EPHESIANS 5:18 KJV**

So, we obviously play a role in being filled with the Spirit. You are filled to the degree you need to be to take the next step. When you properly utilize the Spirit given to you and ask God to increase His presence in you then He will give you more and you can undertake more. By listening to the Holy Spirit in you for your next step and then by trusting in Him to enable you to take that step you conform yourself to God's will. In order to experience this process you must believe that this process is real and ask God for more of His Holy Spirit. Then honor and utilize what He gives you. That's how we fulfill His command to "be filled with the Spirit". As you do this, you demonstrate that you can be trusted with more and more of His Holy Spirit and with tasks that release His power in the here and now. That's why Jesus said:

> **I tell you the truth, anyone who believes in Me will do the same works I have done, and even greater works, because I am going to be with the Father.**
>
> **JOHN 14:12 NLT**

Just before He ascended, Jesus said:

> **Anyone who <u>believes and is baptized</u> will be saved. But anyone who refuses to believe will be condemned.**
>
> **(MARK 16:16 NLT)**

It is important that you be baptized. Baptism is a ritual in which you symbolically bury your "old" self and commemorate the spiritual birth of your "new" self. So, find a group of Christians and ask them to baptize you. If you can't find anyone to baptize you then baptize yourself. Get into a swimming pool or river or bath tub and say: "I renounce Satan and all his wicked works I commit myself to Jesus as my Lord and Savior." Dip yourself under the water and then say: "I Baptize myself in the name of the Father, Son, and Holy Spirit." Now, see yourself as having been washed clean of everything you ever did that offended God.

If you have been "born again" then your "salvation" is secure. You are in right standing before God. In His eyes, you are "righteous". You carry His Holy Spirit with you everywhere you go. It is vitally important that, during The Tribulation, you keep these things in focus.

Chapter 13 is a Verification Checklist. Go there now and check off "I'm a Christian". If you feel like you need more information before making this decision then go to our web site where this book is presented with many links to additional information.

For more information on these topics read this chapter on our web site version and follow the links to the topics of interest.

3

Combat Ready

Paul closes his letter to the church at Ephesus by contrasting the armament of a Roman soldier to five key elements of Christianity.

- Belt > Truth.

- Breast plate > Righteousness.

- Sandals > Readiness.

- Shield > Faith.

- Helmet > Salvation.

- Sword > Scripture.

  (10) A final word: Be strong in the Lord and in His mighty power.

  (11) Put on all of God's armor so that you will be able to stand firm against all strategies of the devil.

  (12) For we are not fighting against flesh-and-blood enemies, but against evil rulers and authorities of the unseen world, against mighty powers in this dark world, and against evil spirits in the heavenly places.

  (13) Therefore, put on every piece of God's armor so you will be able to resist the enemy in the time of evil. Then after the battle you will still be standing firm.

  (14) Stand your ground, putting on the belt of truth and the body armor of God's righteousness.

  (15) For shoes, put on the peace that comes from the Good News so that you will be fully prepared.

(16) In addition to all of these, hold up the shield of faith to stop the fiery arrows of the devil.

(17) Put on salvation as your helmet, and take the sword of the Spirit, which is the word of God.

(18) Pray in the Spirit at all times and on every occasion. Stay alert and be persistent in your prayers for all believers everywhere.

Ephesians 6:10-18 NLT

He uses armor to make a point: Namely, **you are at war!** You are soldiers in a cosmic war between good and evil! The devil really does exist and, when you became a Christian, you defected from his army and you are now in God's army.

Paul put it this way:

(13) For He has rescued us from the kingdom of darkness and transferred us into the Kingdom of His dear Son,

(14) who purchased our freedom [*with His blood*] and forgave our sins.

Colossians 1:13-14 NLT

By becoming a Christian, you openly declared yourself to be Satan's enemy. Now you serve King Jesus and you are a soldier in His army. Satan's soldiers will attempt to maim and kill you.

Speaking of this exact issue, Jesus put it this way:

The thief's purpose is to steal and kill and destroy. My purpose is to give them a rich and satisfying life.

John 10:10 NLT

Since you are alive during The Tribulation, you are engaged in this battle at a level of intensity never before experienced by humans. Therefore, you need to learn how to use the armament God has provided; especially for such a time as this. I do not intend to give you all the ins and outs of Christianity at this time. I intend to help you get through the day.

Verses 10 & 11 tell us that we are to go into battle relying on God's strength and might rather than our own and we are to go wearing the armor God has provided. **Here is a point you will find invaluable. You have been "saved" and your "salvation" is deliverance from every work of the devil, now and forever; but you have a role to play. You, not God, are to put this armor on and use these weapons.** It is not human soldiers, or judges, or officials whom you are at war with: It's the demons who influence and enable them! The armament provided by God is sufficient to overcome the crafty methods of the devil and his army of demons, diminishing the impact they have on you, but you have a role to play. In his commentary on Galatians and Ephesians, the Reformed scholar William Hendriksen explained Ephesians 6:10-18 this way: "…it is even possible to say that not only this or that particular battle but the entire war will be lost unless we exert ourselves. It is true that the counsel of God from eternity will never fail, but it is just as true that in that plan of God from eternity it was decided that victory will be given to those who overcome. Overcomers are conquerors, and in order to conquer one must fight!"

Satan will influence and enable humans to attack you. He appears to some as an angel of light (Second Corinthians 11:14) while convincing others that he does not exist (Acts 20:22). He puts a spin on Bible verses to serve his purpose (Matt. 4:6) and convinces people that wrong is right and right is wrong. To defend yourself against such an enemy and, even more, to go on the offense and take ground, you must learn to use this *spiritual* armament!

Yes, they will come at you physically. But, God has provided for you to overcome the crafty methods of the devil and his army of demons, diminishing the impact they have on you, but you have a role to play. As with any war, every battle begins in the mind. When going into battle, confidence is vitally important. The seventh chapter of Judges tells of the battle of Gilead and how God told Gideon, the commander of His army, to send every soldier home who was "fearful and afraid". God wants only those who trust Him for the victory to engage His enemies in His name. That day at Gilead, two-thirds of the army went home! And today, you too must trust in God to deliver you from your enemies or go home and wait for the enemy to triumph over you and your family. Many will do just that but you don't have to be one of them. That's what "faith" is all about. Faith is not about being a Protestant or a Catholic or such, it's about totally trusting God to do what He has said He will. That's why you need time to study the Bible and get familiar with what He has said and integrate it.

This is why the helmet of salvation is part of your armament. Again, your "salvation" is deliverance from <u>every</u> work of the devil; <u>now</u>, as well as in the future. You don't just wear the helmet of salvation with an eye to eternal bliss but to defend yourself and to advance, taking ground in the here and now! You engage the enemy standing on the promises of God; that He will deliver you from Satan's attacks. Read Psalm 23; slowly! But always remember, you still have to give it all you've got!

The enemy will try to convince you that God cannot be trusted in this way; that you cannot withstand his attacks; that you have no active role in this war and so on and so on.

He will try to convince you that you are not really saved; that you are unworthy of such protection; that your sins will keep you from anything God has to offer; .... That's where the breastplate of righteousness comes in. **Here is another point you will find invaluable. As a Christian, God has made you right with Him. You are in right standing (righteous) with Him.** He no longer holds anything against you. You need to be totally convinced of that or the enemy will use that weakness to defeat you. The last thing Paul says to the Ephesians is:

> **...be kind to each other, tenderhearted, forgiving one another, just as God through Christ has forgiven you.**
>
> **EPHESIANS 4:32 NLT**

John said something similar:

> **I am writing to you who are God's children because your sins have been forgiven through Jesus.**
>
> **1 JOHN 2:12 NLT**

What's more, He has made provision to forgive our sins on an ongoing basis.

> **(8) If we claim we have no sin, we are only fooling ourselves and not living in the truth.**
>
> **(9) But if we confess our sins to Him, He is faithful and just to forgive us our sins and to cleanse us from all wickedness.**
>
> **1 JOHN 1:8-9 NLT**

Even if the enemy knocks you down, God has provided.

> **(14) Is any sick among you? let him call for the elders of the church; and let them pray over him, anointing him with oil in the name of the Lord:**
>
> **(15) And the prayer of faith shall save the sick, and the Lord shall raise him up; and if he have committed sins, they shall be forgiven him.**
>
> **JAMES 5:14-15 KJV**

The point is, **TRUST HIM**. If He says you're forgiven then you are forgiven. If He says He will heal you then He will heal you! And, it is a show of distrust to say otherwise.

So, you need to go into battle each day knowing that you are righteous before God and that He will protect you like a breastplate of armor protected certain vital organs of a Roman soldier.

If you skipped the previous chapter, then go back now and read it! You are in The Tribulation and, you are in no position to skip over anything that relates to your salvation or righteousness. Be absolutely certain that you are born again, and right before God before continuing!

You may have noticed that all of my supporting evidence comes from the Bible. **The words in the Bible are God's words to you**. That's why we call the Bible God's Word. They are the basis of our defense against the enemy. They are also an offensive weapon to be used to attack the enemy. That is why Paul likens them to a sword.

> **For the word of God is alive and powerful. It is sharper than the sharpest two-edged sword, cutting between soul and spirit, between joint and marrow. It exposes our innermost thoughts and desires.**
>
> **HEBREWS 4:12 NLT**

When Jesus was attacked head on by the devil He defended himself with the sword of the Word. Here, the devil begins with a challenge:

(6) and said, "If You are the Son of God, jump off! For the Scriptures say, 'He will order His angels to protect you. And they will hold you up with their hands so you won't even hurt your foot on a stone.'"

(7) Jesus responded, "The Scriptures also say, 'You must not test the LORD your God.'"

(8) Next the devil took Him to the peak of a very high mountain and showed Him all the kingdoms of the world and their glory.

(9) "I will give it all to You," he said, "if You will kneel down and worship me."

(10) "Get out of here, Satan," Jesus told him. "For the Scriptures say, 'You must worship the LORD your God and serve only Him.'"

(11) Then the devil went away, and angels came and took care of Jesus.

MATTHEW 4:6-11 NLT

To follow Jesus' lead in counterattacking Satan, **you have to know God's words and believe God's words and speak God's words from your heart.** Jesus said:

(7) But if you remain in Me and My words remain in you, you may ask for anything you want, and it will be granted!

JOHN 15:7 NLT

We need to buy you as much time as we can; so you can integrate God's words into your character. Paul speaks of the large belt which Roman soldiers wore to protect certain vital organs. The Word of God is truth and when you take it in and are ready to speak it out, then it is as though you had put on one of those big belts like the Roman soldiers wore.

Similarly, when you stand in the knowledge of God's Word and you put your trust in what He says, then it is as if you held up a shield like the ones used by the Romans. Paul says that the flaming arrows of the enemy cannot penetrate the "shield of faith".

Roman soldiers were able to out maneuver their enemies in part because they were equipped with thick soled sandals. They could travel greater distances in a day than their enemies and traverse rougher terrain. A soldier is not ready for battle until he has put on his combat boots! You must be ready to convey the Christian message of the Kingdom of God to a lost and dying world.

The Kingdom of God is here now! Your salvation, deliverance, righteousness, basis for trust in God, are all yours because you were born again, emancipated into the Kingdom of God, and are now committed to defend it against the Kingdom of Satan. Your time is limited, depending on exactly where you are in The Tribulation. You are going to die soon and the only thing you can take with you are the people you bring to The Lord. So, as He commanded, tell others about Him. But, as He also said: "Look, I am sending you out as sheep among wolves. So be as shrewd as snakes and harmless as doves."

Here is the thing; until you are ready for combat, you cannot survive long enough in The Tribulation to be of much use to your king as a warrior.

Knowing His Word and believing it and trusting in Him by acting upon it and expecting results are key to your survival. So, find a Bible and pray for understanding, read it, pray again and reread. Focus initially on the "New Testament" books of Matthew, John, and Acts.

Paul wraps up his presentation on the armor with the following instructions: "Pray in the Spirit at all times and on every occasion. Stay alert and be persistent in your prayers for all believers everywhere." For now, just think of prayer as direct one-on-one real-time communication with God. The most common type of prayer is that in which we ask God for something. Follow these rules:

- Be clear about what you want from God.

- Confirm that what you want is consistent with God's will. Confirm it with corroborating verses from the Bible.

- Ask God in the name of Jesus.

- Believe that God has already granted your request and that the result will materialize in the physical world at any moment. Do not waver.

- Thank God.

- When the result materializes, give Him all the credit.

For more information on these topics read this chapter on our web site version and follow the links to the topics of interest.

4

Kingdom Authority

Every Christian is a citizen in the Kingdom of God; over which Jesus rules as King. Just before Jesus ascended into heaven to await the time set for His physical rule over the earth, He told His disciples:

> **(18) "I have been given all authority in heaven and on earth.**
>
> **(19) Therefore, go and make disciples of all the nations, baptizing them in the name of the Father and the Son and the Holy Spirit.**
>
> **(20) Teach these new disciples to obey all the commands I have given you. And be sure of this: I am with you always, even to the end of the age."**
>
> **MATTHEW 28:18-20 NLT**

In a very real sense, you are a King's Musketeer! But, the Kingdom of God has no territorial boundaries. It exists where ever you go. And, just as a Musketeer exercises authority in the king's name, you exercise authority in Jesus' name.

> **(15) And then He told them, "Go into all the world and preach the Good News to everyone.**
>
> **(16) Anyone who believes and is baptized will be saved. But anyone who refuses to believe will be condemned.**
>
> **(17) These miraculous signs will accompany those who believe: They will cast out demons in My name, and they will speak in new languages.**
>
> **(18) They will be able to handle snakes with safety, and if they drink anything poisonous, it won't hurt them. They will be able to place their hands on the sick, and they will be healed."**

(19) When the Lord Jesus had finished talking with them, He was taken up into heaven and sat down in the place of honor at God's right hand.

(20) And the disciples went everywhere and preached, and the Lord worked through them, confirming what they said by many miraculous signs.

MARK 16:15-20 NLT

The Good News is that we have been emancipated from the kingdom of Satan and made citizens in the Kingdom of God. And, as with any kingdom, certain responsibilities and authority come with citizenship. The most fundamental responsibility of any kingdom is to obey the king. God wants His kingdom to be a huge loving family, over which He is the father. That's why we call Him "Father God". Without the ability to choose to be a member of His family, we would just be robots; not children. But, free will is a double edged sword. In order to have a family of members who freely choose to be part, there must be a provision for them that choose not to. Any action opposed to the king's expressed will is a crime or sin.

Sin distances us from God. He does not want to be in the presence of those who oppose Him. Now, Satan was a powerful angel named Lucifer until he openly rebelled against God and tried to take over the Kingdom of God. Many angels chose to follow him. In response to this sin, this heinous act of treason, a special place called hell was created to contain Satan and his followers.

God is love and Satan's behavior is contrary to love.

But anyone who does not love does not know God, for God is love.

1 JOHN 4:8 NLT

Satan forces those who are not in the Kingdom of God to submit to his rule. His kingdom is called the kingdom of darkness. He uses lies and deception, fear and war, starvation and illness, and such the like, to bring his citizens into submission.

Jesus, referring to Satan as the thief, said:

The thief's purpose is to <u>steal and kill and destroy</u>. My purpose is to give them a rich and satisfying life.

JOHN 10:10 NLT

God lovingly gives and Satan unlovingly takes away. God draws us to Him with love. Satan captures by force. But, God gives us the wherewithal to enter and serve loyally in the Kingdom of God and defend it against Satan and his demon army.

By His divine power, God has given us everything we need for living a godly life. We have received all of this by coming to know Him, the One who called us to Himself by means of His marvelous glory and excellence.

2 PETER 1:3 NLT

His instructions are the Bible. But, as soon as a person receives God's words, Satan comes and tries to steal them so that person won't learn about the Kingdom of God and opt to join.

Referring to God's words as seeds, Jesus said:

> **The seed that fell on the footpath represents those who hear the message about the Kingdom and don't understand it. Then the evil one comes and snatches away the seed that was planted in their hearts.**
>
> **MATTHEW 13:19 NLT**

Here, the person who received God's Word did not even have time to gain an understanding of what was said before Satan came to steal these seeds. Those who resist Satan and gain an understanding of God's Word and opt to join His family and participate in the Kingdom of God, are given authority.

> **And You have caused them to become a Kingdom of priests for our God. And they will reign on the earth."**
>
> **REVELATION 5:10 NLT**

Jesus gives this analogy of His delegation of authority to His followers:

> **"'Well done!' the king exclaimed. 'You are a good servant. You have been faithful with the little 1 entrusted to you, so you will be governor of ten cities as your reward.'"**
>
> **LUKE 19:17 NLT**

When you exercise the authority Jesus has delegated to you, you expand the Kingdom of God on Earth and Satan's army will focus their attention on defeating you. That's why it is so important to understand and utilize the Armor of God presented in Chapter 3. If you didn't read Chapter 3, go back and read it! You have been given authority over Satan and his army of demons. When you direct your attention at them and command them to retreat in the name of King Jesus, they must obey. They will resist, but if you are convinced of your authority and persist, they will retreat.

> **"I tell you the truth, anyone who believes in Me will do the same works I have done, and even greater works, because I am going to be with the Father.**
>
> **JOHN 14:12 NLT**

Whatever the situation, **find verses in the Bible that address the problem and integrate them**. A Bible with a comprehensive concordance and topical index is a good place to start. I have found The New Open Bible – New King James Version – Study Bible published by Nelson to be excellent in this regard. Find out what God's will is for such a situation. Then **take His position and speak His words and believe** they will impact the situation.

Here are a few verses that address various situations to help you understand what I mean. Visit our web site www.FromHereToEternity.info for a wealth of verses presented by category of need.

(7) Go and announce to them that the Kingdom of Heaven is near.

(8) <u>Heal the sick</u>, <u>raise the dead</u>, cure those with leprosy, and <u>cast out demons</u>. Give as freely as you have received!

MATTHEW 10:7-8 NLT

(2) Let all that I am praise the LORD; may I never forget the good things He does for me. (3) He <u>forgives all my sins</u> and <u>heals all my diseases</u>.

PSALMS 103:2-3 NLT

Remember the LORD your God. He is the One who gives you <u>power to be successful</u>, in order to fulfill the covenant He confirmed to your ancestors with an oath.

DEUTERONOMY 8:18 NLT

And this same God who takes care of me will <u>supply all your needs</u> from His glorious riches, which have been given to us in Christ Jesus.

PHILIPPIANS 4:19 NLT

What shall we say about such wonderful things as these? <u>If God is for us, who can ever be against us?</u>

ROMANS 8:31 NLT

(22) Then Jesus said to the disciples, "Have faith in God.

(23) I tell you the truth, you can <u>say to this mountain, 'May you be lifted up and thrown into the sea,' and it will happen</u>. But you must really believe it will happen and have no doubt in your heart.

(24) I tell you, <u>you can pray for anything, and if you believe that you've received it, it will be yours</u>.

(25) But when you are praying, first forgive anyone you are holding a grudge against, so that your Father in heaven will forgive your sins, too. "

MARK 11:22-25 NLT

For I can <u>do everything</u> through Christ, who gives me strength.

PHILIPPIANS 4:13 NLT

5

The Tribulation Timeline

Since you are alive during The Tribulation, it is imperative that you know which events are behind you and which still lie ahead. Your ability to go onward as a Christian soldier largely depends on your ability to anticipate the enemy. The events in the Bible referring to this period are the key! So, I will ferret out certain key events and set them in chronological sequence. We shall refer to the result as **The Tribulation Timeline**.

To show you how this timeline works, examine these two verses.

> **In the beginning God created the heavens and the earth.**
>
> **GENESIS 1:1 NLT**

> **Then I saw a new heaven and a new earth, for the old heaven and the old earth had disappeared. And the sea was also gone.**
>
> **REVELATION 21:1 NLT**

We begin by identifying key events in our Biblical text.

> ➤ (Gen. 1:1) God creates the heavens and the earth.

> ➤ (Rev. 21:1) God recreates the heavens and the earth.

When an event is first placed on the timeline, it will be marked by an arrow. Events already present on the timeline will be marked with a dot; only the new additions will be marked with an arrow.

So, next time we present this timeline, it would appear as follows:

- • (Gen. 1:1) God creates the heavens and the earth.

- ➢ New Event X

- ➢ New Event Y

- ➢ New Event Z

- • (Rev. 21:1) God recreates the heavens and the earth.

We will use one simple rule: **No event appears on the timeline unless it is extracted directly from the Bible**.

Each chapter that follows will take a relevant quotation from the Bible and develop timeline entries from it. Then, those entries will be merged into a composit timeline

If you have questions about any of these events or the way they are presented then go to our web site and examine the chapter in the on-line version. The on-line version contains a wealth of links to in depth information about the points made in this book. It also contains charts to help you visualize the timeline.

The purpose of this timeline is to give you an easy to follow sequence of events to use in determining where in The Tribulation you are and what happens next so that you can successfully engage the enemy.

6

The Tribulation Timeline

from Daniel 9:27

The lynch pin of The Tribulation is the work of the Antichrist and his most significant actions take place in the middle of The Tribulation. So, we will develop our timeline by starting in the middle and moving out to the beginning and end.

Daniel wrote that an angel spoke with him saying:

> **The ruler will make a treaty with the people for a period of one set of seven, but after half this time, he will put an end to the sacrifices and offerings. And as a climax to all his terrible deeds, he will set up a sacrilegious object that causes desecration, until the fate decreed for this defiler is finally poured out on him."**
>
> **DANIEL 9:27 NLT**

When Daniel says "one set of seven" he means 7 years.

The original text says that this ruler will "confirm a covenant with many". The implication is that this treaty already exists and this ruler is committing to see that it is upheld for 7 years.

This agreement has always been understood to be with the nation of Israel and this "ruler" has been understood to be "the Antichrist".

We can chart these events as follows:

- ➢ (Dan. 9:27) A "ruler", the Antichrist, makes a 7 year agreement which, it would seem, protects the right of Israel to conduct Levitical sacrificial worship at the temple in Jerusalem

- ➢ (Dan. 9:27) After half of this 7 year agreement, the Antichrist breaks this agreement by stopping the Levitical worship at the temple.

➢ (Dan. 9:27) The Antichrist sets up a sacrilegious object that desecrates the temple. It remains until his demise.

➢ (Dan. 9:27) The fate decreed for the Antichrist is poured out on him.

Now, for any of this to happen, the Antichrist has to have risen to such a powerful position as a "ruler" that he can make such a guarantee to Israel. At the time this was written, the temple in Jerusalem did not exist. The temple mount is a holy place to Muslims. Islamic sentiment prohibits the construction there of a Jewish temple. However, for this ruler to "put an end to the sacrifices and offerings" there must first be such a temple on the temple mount in Jerusalem and the Levitical sacrificial worship system must have been reinstated. Therefore, either the Islamic sentiment has been neutralized or this ruler is so powerful that he can decree such a thing and Muslims the world over will comply.

The Tribulation is also known as the time of Jacob's Trouble. Jacob had to work for Laban (Genesis 29) for 7 years in order to marry his daughter. Laban deceived Jacob and, the "trouble" was, Jacob had to work another 7 years.

The prophet Jeremiah (30:7) said that after God establishes a new state of Israel and brings the Jews back from all over the world that a time of great distress will precede the coming of the Messiah. Jeremiah referred to it as "the time of Jacob's trouble". Jewish scholars have always taken this to be a seven year period. Since Jesus referred to this period as The Tribulation; it is seen as overlapping the time of Jacob's trouble and the Antichrist's seven year agreement.

The Tribulation is reckoned to begin at the time of the agreement made by the Antichrist and The Great Tribulation is reckoned to begin with his breaking of this same agreement.

❖ Antichrist makes/confirms 7 year agreement/covenant.

❖ **The Tribulation has begun.**

❖ Antichrist breaks agreement after 3 ½ years.

❖ Antichrist stops worship sacrifices and offerings at the temple in Jerusalem.

❖ Antichrist desecrates temple.

❖ **The Great Tribulation has begun**.

❖ 3 ½ years later the Antichrist is thrown into the lake of fire.

If such an agreement has already been made then you are indeed in The Tribulation. So, go to the Chapter 13 Verification Checklist and check "I'm in The Tribulation. Further, if midway that agreement was broken and the one who made it stopped the sacrificial services at the temple then you are in The Great Tribulation. Return to Chapter 13 and check "I'm in The Great Tribulation".

7

The Tribulation Timeline

from Matthew 24:1-31

Since Matt. 24:21 & 22 were used to establish a working definition of The Great Tribulation, we shall include them early on. However, verses 1-31 set the context in which Jesus spoke of The Great Tribulation; plus they are key to your understanding of the order in which events have occurred and will occur. So, read the following slowly and carefully!

(1) As Jesus was leaving the Temple grounds, His disciples pointed out to Him the various Temple buildings.

(2) But He responded, "Do you see all these buildings? I tell you the truth, they will be completely demolished. Not one stone will be left on top of another!"

(3) Later, Jesus sat on the Mount of Olives. His disciples came to Him privately and said, "Tell us, when will all this happen? What sign will signal Your return and the end of the world? "

(4) Jesus told them, "Don't let anyone mislead you,

(5) for many will come in My name, claiming, 'I am the Messiah.' They will deceive many.

(6) And you will hear of wars and threats of wars, but don't panic. Yes, these things must take place, but the end won't follow immediately.

(7) Nation will go to war against nation, and kingdom against kingdom. There will be famines and earthquakes in many parts of the world.

(8) But all this is only the first of the birth pains, with more to come.

(9) "Then you will be arrested, persecuted, and killed. You will be hated all over the world because you are My followers.

(10) And many will turn away from Me and betray and hate each other.

(11) And many false prophets will appear and will deceive many people.

(12) Sin will be rampant everywhere, and the love of many will grow cold.

(13) But the one who endures to the end will be saved.

(14) And the Good News about the Kingdom will be preached throughout the whole world, so that all nations will hear it; and then the end will come.

(15) "The day is coming when you will see what Daniel the prophet spoke about—the sacrilegious object that causes desecration standing in the Holy Place." (Reader, pay attention!)

(16) "Then those in Judea must flee to the hills.

(17) A person out on the deck of a roof must not go down into the house to pack.

(18) A person out in the field must not return even to get a coat.

(19) How terrible it will be for pregnant women and for nursing mothers in those days.

(20) And pray that your flight will not be in winter or on the Sabbath.

(21) For there will be greater anguish than at any time since the world began. And it will never be so great again.

(22) In fact, unless that time of calamity is shortened, not a single person will survive. But it will be shortened for the sake of God's chosen ones.

(23) "Then if anyone tells you, 'Look, here is the Messiah,' or 'There he is,' don't believe it.

(24) For false messiahs and false prophets will rise up and perform great signs and wonders so as to deceive, if possible, even God's chosen ones.

(25) See, I have warned you about this ahead of time.

(26) "So if someone tells you, 'Look, the Messiah is out in the desert,' don't bother to go and look. Or, 'Look, he is hiding here,' don't believe it!

(27) For as the lightning flashes in the east and shines to the west, so it will be when the Son of Man comes.

(28) Just as the gathering of vultures shows there is a carcass nearby, so these signs indicate that the end is near.

(29) "Immediately after the anguish of those days, the sun will be darkened, the moon will give no light, the stars will fall from the sky, and the powers in the heavens will be shaken.

(30) And then at last, the sign that the Son of Man is coming will appear in the heavens, and there will be deep mourning among all the peoples of the earth. And they will see the Son of Man coming on the clouds of heaven with power and great glory.

(31) And He will send out His angels with the mighty blast of a trumpet, and they will gather His chosen ones from all over the world—from the farthest ends of the earth and heaven.

MATTHEW 24:1-31 NLT

You will recall that the term "great tribulation" is ***megas thlipsis*** in the original Greek text. The translators of this New Living Translation (NLT) above, translated the Greek expression ***megas thlipsis*** in verse 21 as "greater anguish" rather than "great tribulation" simply to express the thought in a more contemporary way. Never the less, the time referenced is the ***megas thlipsis*** or Great Tribulation. Essentially, Jesus coined the expression Great Tribulation.

Note that the four catastrophic events in Verse 29 occur "immediately after" The Great Tribulation but <u>before</u> He returns.

Also note that the sign of His return is witnessed globally and even causes unbelievers worldwide to mourn the error of their ways (verse 30).

Now, from Matthew 24:1-31 we shall extract these events:

- ➢ (Matt. 24:2) Destruction of the temple in Jerusalem.

- ➢ (Matt. 24:5) Many will come claiming to be "the Christ" and deceiving many.

- ➢ (Matt 24:6) Hear of wars and rumors of wars <u>but end is not yet</u>.

- ➢ (Matt. 24:7) Nation rises against nation and kingdom against kingdom.

- ➢ (Matt. 24:7) Famines, plagues, and earthquakes around the world.

- ➢ (Matt 24:8) Jesus refers to the events of verses 5-7 as birth pangs.

- ➢ (Matt. 24:9) Christians persecuted and martyred.

- ➢ (Matt. 24:10) Many Christians lose their faith in Christ due to persecution.

- ➢ (Matt. 24:11) Many false prophets will rise up and deceive many.

- ➢ (Matt. 24:12) Love will wax cold for many.

- ➢ (Matt. 24:15) Gospel preached in all the world. Then <u>"after that" the end will come.</u>

- ➢ (Matt. 24:15) The abomination of desolation (aka "a sacrilegious object" in Daniel 9:27) stands in the holy place.

- ➢ **(Matt. 24:21) The Great Tribulation begins.**

- ➢ (Matt. 24:21) The events occurring during this period are worse than anything that has ever happened or ever will again.

- ➢ (Matt. 24:24) False Christs & false prophets show great signs & wonders.

➢ **(Matt. 24:29) The Great Tribulation ends.**

➢ (Matt. 24:29) "Immediately after" The Tribulation, the sun will be darkened, the moon will give no light, the stars will fall from the sky, and the powers in the heavens will be shaken.

➢ (Matt. 24:30) "Then" the sign of Jesus' return appears in the sky.

➢ (Matt. 24:30) The unbelievers on earth will mourn and see Jesus returning with power and great glory.

➢ (Matt. 24:31) There will be a great trumpet blast.

➢ (Matt. 24:31) His angels gather all the believers from everywhere; earth and heaven.

Now let's merge these events with those already on our timeline.

➢ (Matt. 24:2) Destruction of the temple in Jerusalem.

➢ (Matt. 24:5) Many will come claiming to be "the Christ" and deceiving many.

➢ (Matt 24:6) Hear of wars and rumors of wars but end is not yet.

➢ (Matt 24:7) Nation rises against nation and kingdom against kingdom.

➢ (Matt 24:7) Famines, plagues, and earthquakes around the world.

➢ (Matt 24:8) Jesus refers to the events of verses 5-7 as birth pangs.

➢ (Matt. 24:9) Christians persecuted and martyred.

➢ (Matt. 24:10) Many Christians lose their faith in Christ due to persecution.

➢ (Matt. 24:11) Many false prophets will rise up and deceive many.

➢ (Matt. 24:12) Love will wax cold for many.

❖ **The Tribulation begins**

• (Dan. 9:27) A "ruler", the Antichrist, makes a 7 year agreement which, it would seem, protects the right of Israel to conduct Levitical sacrificial worship at the temple in Jerusalem.

• (Dan. 9:27) After half of this 7 year agreement, the Antichrist breaks this agreement by stopping the Levitical worship at the temple.

➢ **(Matt. 24:21) The Great Tribulation begins.**

• *(Dan. 9:27) The Antichrist sets up a sacrilegious object that desecrates the temple. It remains until his demise.*

➢ *(Matt. 24:15) The abomination of desolation stands in the holy place.*

➢ (Matt. 24:15) Gospel preached in all the world. Then <u>"after that" the end will come.</u>

➢ (Matt. 24:21) The events occurring during this period are worse than anything that has ever happened or ever will again.

➢ (Matt. 24:24) False Christs & false prophets show great signs & wonders.

➢ **(Matt. 24:29) The Great Tribulation ends.**

➢ (Matt. 24:29) "Immediately after" The Tribulation, the sun will be darkened, the moon will give no light, the stars will fall from the sky, and the powers in the heavens will be shaken.

➢ (Matt. 24:30) "Then" the sign of Jesus' return appears in the sky.

➢ (Matt. 24:30) The unbelievers on earth will mourn and see Jesus returning with power and great glory.

➢ (Matt. 24:31) There will be a great trumpet blast.

➢ (Matt. 24:31) His angels gather all the believers from everywhere; earth and heaven.

• (Dan. 9:27) The fate decreed for the Antichrist is poured out on him.

So, if such a 7 year agreement has been made then you are indeed in The Tribulation. Go to the Checklist in Chapter 13 and check "I'm in The Tribulation. Further, if midway in that 7 year agreement it was broken and the one who made it has stopped the worship services at the temple then you are in The Great Tribulation. Return to the checklist and check "I'm in The Great Tribulation".

As you can see, I am using the term "The Great Tribulation" as the key event in the timeline. It marks the point at which the Antichrist desecrates the Jewish temple in Jerusalem. Hence, Matthew 24:15 and Daniel 9:27 intersect at this point. See italicized verses.

8

The Tribulation Timeline

from 2ⁿᵈ Thessalonians 2:1-11

(1) Now, dear brothers and sisters, let us clarify some things about the coming of our Lord Jesus Christ and how we will be gathered to meet Him.

(2) Don't be so easily shaken or alarmed by those who say that the day of the Lord has already begun. Don't believe them, even if they claim to have had a spiritual vision, a revelation, or a letter supposedly from us.

(3) Don't be fooled by what they say. <u>For that day will not come until there is a great rebellion against God and the man of lawlessness is revealed—the one who brings destruction.</u>

(4) He will <u>exalt himself</u> and <u>defy everything that people call god</u> and every object of worship. He will even <u>sit in the temple of God, claiming that he himself is God.</u>

(5) Don't you remember that I told you about all this when I was with you?

(6) And you know what is holding him back, for he can be revealed only when his time comes.

(7) For this lawlessness is already at work secretly, and it will remain secret until the one who is holding it back steps out of the way.

(8) Then the man of lawlessness will be revealed, but the Lord Jesus will kill him with the breath of His mouth and destroy him by the splendor of His coming.

(9) This man will come to do the work of Satan with counterfeit power and signs and miracles.

(10) He will use every kind of evil deception to fool those on their way to destruction, because they refuse to love and accept the truth that would save them.

(11) So God will cause them to be greatly deceived, and they will believe these lies.

2 Thessalonians 2:1-11 NLT

Now, let's extract the tribulation events.

- ➤ (2nd Thes 2:3) The great rebellion against God occurs.

- ➤ (2nd Thes 2:7) He who or that which restrains the Antichrist is removed or is no longer blocking his way.

- ➤ (2nd Thes 2:3) The Antichrist or man of lawlessness is revealed.

- ➤ (2nd Thes 2:4) The Antichrist sits down in "the temple of God" proclaiming that he is God.

- ➤ (2nd Thes 2:9) Satan empowers the Antichrist to perform signs and miracles.

- ➤ (2nd Thes 2:11) God enables those who believe the Antichrist to sink deep into their delusions.

- ➤ (2nd Thes 2:11) Upon His return, Jesus kills the Antichrist.

Now, we shall integrate these events into our timeline.

- • (Matt. 24:2) Destruction of the temple in Jerusalem.

- • (Matt. 24:5) Many will come claiming to be "the Christ" and deceiving many.

- • (Matt 24:6) Hear of wars and rumors of wars but end is not yet.

- • (Matt 24:7) Nation rises against nation and kingdom against kingdom.

- • (Matt. 24:7) Famines, plagues, and earthquakes around the world.

- • (Matt 24:8) Jesus refers to the events of verses 5-7 as birth pangs.

- • (Matt. 24:9) Christians persecuted and martyred.

- • (Matt. 24:10) Many Christians lose their faith in Christ due to persecution.

- • (Matt. 24:11) Many false prophets will rise up and deceive many.

- • (Matt. 24:12) Love will wax cold for many.

- • **The Tribulation begins**

- ➤ (2nd Thes 2:3) The great rebellion against God occurs.

- ➤ (2nd Thes 2:7) He who or that which restrains the Antichrist is removed or is no longer blocking his way.

- ➤ (2nd Thes 2:3) The Antichrist or man of lawlessness is revealed

- (Dan. 9:27) A "ruler", the Antichrist, makes a 7 year agreement which, it would seem, protects the right of Israel to conduct Levitical sacrificial worship at the temple in Jerusalem.

- (Dan. 9:27) After half of this 7 year agreement, the Antichrist breaks this agreement by stopping the Levitical worship at the temple.

- **(Matt. 24:21) The Great Tribulation begins.**

➢ (2nd Thes 2:4) The Antichrist sits down in "the temple of God" proclaiming that he is God.

➢ (2nd Thes 2:9) Satan empowers the Antichrist to perform signs and miracles.

- (Dan. 9:27) The Antichrist sets up a sacrilegious object that desecrates the temple. It remains until his demise.

- (Matt. 24:15) Gospel preached in all the world. Then <u>"after that" the end will come</u>.

- (Matt. 24:15) The abomination of desolation stands in the holy place.

- (Matt. 24:21) The events occurring during this period are worse than anything that has ever happened or ever will again.

- *(Matt. 24:24) False Christs & false prophets show great signs & wonders.*

➢ *(2nd Thes 2:11) God enables those who believe the Antichrist to sink deep into their delusions.*

- **(Matt. 24:29) The Great Tribulation ends.**

- (Matt. 24:29) "Immediately after" The Tribulation, the sun will be darkened, the moon will give no light, the stars will fall from the sky, and the powers in the heavens will be shaken.

- (Matt. 24:30) "Then" the sign of Jesus' return appears in the sky.

- (Matt. 24:30) The unbelievers on earth will mourn and see Jesus returning with power and great glory.

- (Matt. 24:31) There will be a great trumpet blast.

- (Matt. 24:31) His angels gather all the believers from everywhere; earth and heaven.

- (Dan. 9:27) The fate decreed for the Antichrist is poured out on him.

➢ (2nd Thes 2:11) Upon His return, Jesus kills the Antichrist.

Regardless of when The Tribulation begins, 2nd Thes. 2:1-11 coincides with Daniel 9:27. Both address the rule of the Antichrist from his rise to power to his demise. Hence, they are positioned adjacent to each other except for the 2nd Thes. 2:11 reference to the delusional aspect of the Antichrist's followers. This aspect fits best after Matthew 24:24 regarding Satan's empowerment of the Antichrist to demonstrate signs and wonders/miracles. See italicized verses.

9

The Tribulation Timeline

from Daniel 12:11

"From the time the daily sacrifice is stopped and the sacrilegious object that causes desecration is set up to be worshiped, there will be 1,290 days

DANIEL 12:11 NLT

1290 days is 3.5 years plus 30 days.

Event extracted from Daniel 12:11

➤ (Dan. 12:11) From the time the Antichrist halts the Levitical worship there will be 1,290 days; or 3 ½ years plus 30 days.

Merging these events into the Tribulation Timeline

- (Matt. 24:2) Destruction of the temple in Jerusalem.

- (Matt. 24:5) Many will come claiming to be "the Christ" and deceiving many.

- (Matt 24:6) Hear of wars and rumors of wars but end is not yet.

- (Matt 24:7) Nation rises against nation and kingdom against kingdom.

- (Matt 24:7) Famines, plagues, and earthquakes around the world.

- (Matt 24:8) Jesus refers to the events of verses 5-7 as birth pangs.

- (Matt 24:9) Christians persecuted and martyred.

- (Matt. 24:10) Many Christians lose their faith in Christ due to persecution.

- (Matt. 24:11) Many false prophets will rise up and deceive many.

- (Matt. 24:12) Love will wax cold for many.

❖ **The Tribulation begins**

- (2nd Thes 2:3) The great rebellion against God occurs.

- (2nd Thes 2:7) He who or that which restrains the Antichrist is removed or is no longer blocking his way.

- (2nd Thes 2:3) The Antichrist or man of lawlessness is revealed

- (Dan. 9:27) A "ruler", the Antichrist, makes a 7 year agreement which, it would seem, protects the right of Israel to conduct Levitical sacrificial worship at the temple in Jerusalem.

- *(Dan. 9:27) After half of this 7 year agreement, the Antichrist breaks this agreement by stopping the Levitical worship at the temple.*

- **(Matt. 24:21) The Great Tribulation begins.**

➤ *(Dan. 12:11) From the time the Antichrist halts the Levitical worship there will be 1,290 days; or 3 ½ years plus 30 days.*

- (2nd Thes 2:4) The Antichrist sits down in "the temple of God" proclaiming that he is God.

- (2nd Thes 2:9) Satan empowers the Antichrist to perform signs and miracles.

- (Dan. 9:27) The Antichrist sets up a sacrilegious object that desecrates the temple. It remains until his demise.

- (Matt. 24:15) Gospel preached in all the world. Then "after that" the end will come.

- (Matt. 24:15) The abomination of desolation stands in the holy place.

- (Matt. 24:21) The events occurring during this period are worse than anything that has ever happened or ever will again.

- (Matt. 24:24) False Christs & false prophets show great signs & wonders.

- (2nd Thes 2:11) God enables those who believe the Antichrist to sink deep into their delusions.

- **(Matt. 24:29) The Great Tribulation ends.**

- (Matt. 24:29) "Immediately after" The Tribulation, the sun will be darkened, the moon will give no light, the stars will fall from the sky, and the powers in the heavens will be shaken.

- (Matt. 24:30) "Then" the sign of Jesus' return appears in the sky.

- (Matt. 24:30) The unbelievers on earth will mourn and see Jesus returning with power and great glory.

- (Matt. 24:31) There will be a great trumpet blast.

- (Matt. 24:31) His angels gather all the believers from everywhere; earth and heaven.

- (Dan. 9:27) The fate decreed for the Antichrist is poured out on him.

- (2nd Thes 2:11) Upon His return, Jesus kills the Antichrist.

The fact that Daniel 12:11 and 9:27 both refer to the Antichrist causing the worship services at the temple be halted puts them together on the timeline. See italicized verses.

10

The Tribulation Timeline

from Revelation 13

(1) Then the dragon took his stand on the shore beside the sea. Then I saw a beast rising up out of the sea. It had seven heads and ten horns, with ten crowns on its horns. And written on each head were names that blasphemed God.

(2) This beast looked like a leopard, but it had the feet of a bear and the mouth of a lion! And the dragon gave the beast his own power and throne and great authority.

(3) I saw that one of the heads of the beast seemed wounded beyond recovery—but the fatal wound was healed! The whole world marveled at this miracle and gave allegiance to the beast.

(4) They worshiped the dragon for giving the beast such power, and they also worshiped the beast. "Who is as great as the beast?" they exclaimed. "Who is able to fight against him?"

(5) Then the beast was allowed to speak great blasphemies against God. And he was given authority to do whatever he wanted for forty-two months.

(6) And he spoke terrible words of blasphemy against God, slandering His name and His dwelling—that is, those who dwell in heaven.

(7) And the beast was allowed to wage war against God's holy people and to conquer them. And he was given authority to rule over every tribe and people and language and nation.

(8) And all the people who belong to this world worshiped the beast. They are the ones whose names were not written in the Book of Life before the world was made—the Book that belongs to the Lamb who was slaughtered.

(9) Anyone with ears to hear should listen and understand.

(10) Anyone who is destined for prison will be taken to prison. Anyone destined to die by the sword will die by the sword. This means that God's holy people must endure persecution patiently and remain faithful.

(11) Then I saw another beast come up out of the earth. He had two horns like those of a lamb, but he spoke with the voice of a dragon.

(12) He exercised all the authority of the first beast. And he required all the earth and its people to worship the first beast, whose fatal wound had been healed.

(13) He did astounding miracles, even making fire flash down to earth from the sky while everyone was watching.

(14) And with all the miracles he was allowed to perform on behalf of the first beast, he deceived all the people who belong to this world. He ordered the people to make a great statue of the first beast, who was fatally wounded and then came back to life.

(15) He was then permitted to give life to this statue so that it could speak. Then the statue of the beast commanded that anyone refusing to worship it must die.

(16) He required everyone—small and great, rich and poor, free and slave—to be given a mark on the right hand or on the forehead.

(17) And no one could buy or sell anything without that mark, which was either the name of the beast or the number representing his name.

(18) Wisdom is needed here. Let the one with understanding solve the meaning of the number of the beast, for it is the number of a man. His number is 666.

Revelation 13:1-18 NLT

Extracted events:

➢ (Rev. 13:1) Man of lawlessness/the beast/the Antichrist is revealed.

➢ (Rev. 13:1) Beast/Antichrist has 7 heads and 10 horns.

➢ (Rev. 13:2) Satan empowers the Antichrist.

➢ (Rev. 13:3) Antichrist recovers from the fatal head wound. See also verses 12 and 14.

➢ (Rev. 13:4) People worship Satan who empowered the Antichrist.

➢ (Rev. 13:4) People worship the Antichrist.

➢ (Rev. 13:5) Antichrist can do whatever he wants for 3 ½ years.

➢ (Rev. 13:5) Antichrist blasphemes God.

➢ (Rev. 13:7) Antichrist wages war on Christians and overcomes them.

➢ (Rev. 13:11) Antichrist is joined by "another beast"; aka "the false prophet".

- ➤ (Rev. 13:12) False prophet is given all the authority of the Antichrist.

- ➤ (Rev. 13:12) False prophet requires people to worship the Antichrist.

- ➤ (Rev. 13:13) False prophet performs miracles.

- ➤ (Rev. 13:14) With miracles he deceives many, the world over.

- ➤ (Rev. 13:14) False prophet has a statue of the Antichrist made.

- ➤ (Rev. 13:15) False prophet "gives life to the statue" which speaks.

- ➤ (Rev. 13:15) The statue commands that anyone refusing to worship it be executed.

- ➤ (Rev. 13:16) All who will not receive "the mark" of the Antichrist are executed.

- ➤ (Rev. 13:17) Only those with the mark of the Antichrist on their forehead or right side can buy or sell.

Integration of events into The Tribulation Timeline

- (Matt. 24:2) Destruction of the temple in Jerusalem.

- (Matt. 24:5) Many will come claiming to be "the Christ" and deceiving many.

- (Matt 24:6) Hear of wars and rumors of wars but end is not yet.

- (Matt 24:7) Nation rises against nation and kingdom against kingdom.

- (Matt. 24:7) Famines, plagues, and earthquakes around the world.

- (Matt 24:8) Jesus refers to the events of verses 5-7 as birth pangs.

- (Matt. 24:9) Christians persecuted and martyred.

- (Matt. 24:10) Many Christians lose their faith in Christ due to persecution.

- (Matt. 24:11) Many false prophets will rise up and deceive many.

- (Matt. 24:12) Love will wax cold for many.

- ❖ **The Tribulation begins**

- (2nd Thes 2:3) The great rebellion against God occurs.

- (2nd Thes 2:7) He who or that which restrains the Antichrist is removed or is no longer blocking his way.

- *(2nd Thes 2:3) The Antichrist or man of lawlessness is revealed.*

- (Dan. 9:27) A "ruler", the Antichrist, makes a 7 year agreement which, it would seem, protects the right of Israel to conduct Levitical sacrificial worship at the temple in Jerusalem.

- ➤ *(Rev. 13:1) Man of lawlessness/the beast/the Antichrist is revealed.*

- ➤ (Rev. 13:1) Beast/Antichrist has 7 heads and 10 horns.

- ➤ (Rev. 13:2) Satan empowers the Antichrist.

- ➤ *(Rev. 13:3) Antichrist recovers from the fatal head wound. See also verses 12 and 14.*

- • *(Dan. 9:27) After half of this 7 year agreement, the Antichrist breaks this agreement by stopping the Levitical worship at the temple.*

- • **(Matt. 24:21) The Great Tribulation begins.**

- • (Dan. 12:11) From the time the Antichrist halts the Levitical worship there will be 1,290 days; or 3 ½ years plus 30 days.

- ➤ (Rev. 13:4) People worship Satan who empowered the Antichrist.

- ➤ (Rev. 13:4) People worship the Antichrist.

- ➤ (Rev. 13:5) Antichrist can do whatever he wants for 3 ½ years.

- ➤ (Rev. 13:5) Antichrist blasphemes God.

- ➤ (Rev. 13:7) Antichrist wages war on Christians and overcomes them.

- ➤ (Rev. 13:11) Antichrist is joined by "another beast"; aka "the false prophet".

- ➤ (Rev. 13:12) False prophet is given all the authority of the Antichrist.

- ➤ (Rev. 13:12) False prophet requires people to worship the Antichrist.

- ➤ (Rev. 13:13) False prophet performs miracles.

- ➤ (Rev. 13:14) With miracles he deceives many, the world over.

- • (2nd Thes 2:4) The Antichrist sits down in "the temple of God" proclaiming that he is God.

- • (2nd Thes 2:9) Satan empowers the Antichrist to perform signs and miracles.

- • (Dan. 9:27) The Antichrist sets up a sacrilegious object that desecrates the temple. It remains until his demise.

- • (Matt. 24:15) Gospel preached in all the world. Then <u>"after that" the end will come.</u>

- • (Matt. 24:15) The abomination of desolation stands in the holy place.

- • (Matt. 24:21) The events occurring during this period are worse than anything that has ever happened or ever will again.

- ➤ (Rev. 13:14) False prophet has a statue of the Antichrist made.

➤ (Rev. 13:15) False prophet "gives life to the statue" which speaks.

➤ (Rev. 13:15) The statue commands that anyone refusing to worship it be executed.

➤ (Rev. 13:16) All who will not receive "the mark" of the Antichrist are executed.

➤ (Rev. 13:17) Only those with the mark of the Antichrist on their forehead or right side can buy or sell.

• (Matt. 24:24) False Christs & false prophets show great signs & wonders.

• (2nd Thes 2:11) God enables those who believe the Antichrist to sink deep into their delusions.

• **(Matt. 24:29) The Great Tribulation ends.**

• (Matt. 24:29) "Immediately after" The Tribulation, the sun will be darkened, the moon will give no light, the stars will fall from the sky, and the powers in the heavens will be shaken.

• (Matt. 24:30) "Then" the sign of Jesus' return appears in the sky.

• (Matt. 24:30) The unbelievers on earth will mourn and see Jesus returning with power and great glory.

• (Matt. 24:31) There will be a great trumpet blast.

• (Matt. 24:31) His angels gather all the believers from everywhere; earth and heaven.

• (Dan. 9:27) The fate decreed for the Antichrist is poured out on him.

• (2nd Thes 2:11) Upon His return, Jesus kills the Antichrist.

These are many of the main events of The Great Tribulation. If the events of Matthew 24:29 have occurred then The Great Tribulation is over and you will see the sign of Jesus' return any day now. So, hang on! Listen for the sound of the trumpet!

Rev. 13:1 correlates directly with 2nd Thes. 2:11. See italicized verses.

Rev. 13:2-3 correlate to Dan. 9:27 when the Antichrist seems to move from a position of leadership to a tyrannical position of dominance. See italicized verses.

Rev. 13:4-17 speak of his domination during the last 3 ½ years of his life. Hence, they fit quite well in the period referred to as The Great Tribulation. Verses 14-17 address his dominance as it operates during this 3 ½ year period.

11

The Tribulation Timeline

from Revelation 6

(1) As I watched, the Lamb broke the first of the seven seals on the scroll. Then I heard one of the four living beings say with a voice like thunder, "Come!"

(2) I looked up and saw a white horse standing there. Its rider carried a bow, and a crown was placed on his head. He rode out to win many battles and gain the victory.

(3) When the Lamb broke the second seal, I heard the second living being say, "Come!"

(4) Then another horse appeared, a red one. Its rider was given a mighty sword and the authority to take peace from the earth. And there was war and slaughter everywhere.

(5) When the Lamb broke the third seal, I heard the third living being say, "Come!" I looked up and saw a black horse, and its rider was holding a pair of scales in his hand.

(6) And I heard a voice from among the four living beings say, "A loaf of wheat bread or three loaves of barley will cost a day's pay. And don't waste the olive oil and wine."

(7) When the Lamb broke the fourth seal, I heard the fourth living being say, "Come!"

(8) I looked up and saw a horse whose color was pale green. Its rider was named Death, and his companion was the Grave. These two were given authority over one-fourth of the earth, to kill with the sword and famine and disease and wild animals.

(9) When the Lamb broke the fifth seal, I saw under the altar the souls of all who had been martyred for the word of God and for being faithful in their testimony.

(10) They shouted to the Lord and said, "O Sovereign Lord, holy and true, how long before You judge the people who belong to this world and avenge our blood for what they have done to us?"

(11) Then a white robe was given to each of them. And they were told to rest a little longer until the full number of their brothers and sisters—their fellow servants of Jesus who were to be martyred—had joined them.

(12) I watched as the Lamb broke the sixth seal, and there was a great earthquake. The sun became as dark as black cloth, and the moon became as red as blood.

(13) Then the stars of the sky fell to the earth like green figs falling from a tree shaken by a strong wind.

(14) The sky was rolled up like a scroll, and all of the mountains and islands were moved from their places.

(15) Then everyone—the kings of the earth, the rulers, the generals, the wealthy, the powerful, and every slave and free person—all hid themselves in the caves and among the rocks of the mountains.

(16) And they cried to the mountains and the rocks, "Fall on us and hide us from the face of the One who sits on the throne and from the wrath of the Lamb.

(17) For the great day of their wrath has come, and who is able to survive?"

REVELATION 6:1-17 NLT

Extracted events:

- ➤ (Rev. 6:1) *Jesus breaks the first seal*
- ➤ (Rev. 6:2) The Antichrist has authority and conquers with the threat of war.
- ➤ (Rev. 6:3) *Jesus breaks the second seal*
- ➤ (Rev. 6:4) There is "war and slaughter everywhere".
- ➤ (Rev. 6:4) *Jesus breaks the third seal*
- ➤ (Rev. 6:6) Famine ensues such that a day's wage just pays for your
- ➤ meals. But the rich and powerful continue to live well.
- ➤ (Rev. 6:7) *Jesus breaks the forth seal*
- ➤ (Rev. 6:8) Wars, famine, and disease consume ¼ of the world.
- ➤ (Rev. 6:9) *Jesus breaks the fifth seal*
- ➤ (Rev. 6:9-11) More Christians are yet to be martyred.
- ➤ (Rev. 6:12) *Jesus breaks the sixth seal*
- ➤ (Rev. 6:12) There is a great earthquake.
- ➤ (Rev. 6:12) The sun becomes dark as black cloth.

➢ (Rev. 6:12) The moon becomes blood red.

➢ (Rev. 6:13) Asters (glowing objects) fall from the sky.

➢ (Rev. 6:14) The sky rolls up like a scroll.

➢ (Rev. 6:14) Islands and mountains are moved.

➢ (Rev. 6:15) People everywhere hide.

➢ (Rev. 6:9) People everywhere ask for death.

➢ (Rev. 6:16-17) People say they are experiencing the wrath of Christ and of God the Father.

Note that the sequence of events presented in verses 12-14 parallel those Jesus said would mark the termination of The Great Tribulation.

> **Immediately after the tribulation of those days shall the sun be darkened, and the moon shall not give her light, and the stars shall fall from heaven, and the powers of the heavens shall be shaken:**
>
> **MATTHEW 24:29 KJV**

Chapter 6 of the Revelation closes with survivors proclaiming that they are experiencing the wrath of Christ and God the Father. The events which follow the breaking of the 7th seal are discussed in depth on our web site.

An integrated list is as follows:

• (Matt. 24:2) Destruction of the temple in Jerusalem.

• (Matt. 24:5) Many will come claiming to be "the Christ" and deceiving many.

• (Matt 24:6) Hear of wars and rumors of wars but end is not yet.

• (Matt 24:7) Nation rises against nation and kingdom against kingdom.

• (Matt. 24:7) Famines, plagues, and earthquakes around the world.

• (Matt 24:8) Jesus refers to the events of verses 5-7 as birth pangs.

• (Matt. 24:9) Christians persecuted and martyred.

• (Matt. 24:10) Many Christians lose their faith in Christ due to persecution.

• (Matt. 24:11) Many false prophets will rise up and deceive many.

    (Matt. 24:12) Love will wax cold for many.

❖ **The Tribulation begins**

• (2nd Thes 2:3) The great rebellion against God occurs.

- (2nd Thes 2:7) He who or that which restrains the Antichrist is removed or is no longer blocking his way.

- (2nd Thes 2:3) The Antichrist or man of lawlessness is revealed.

- (Dan. 9:27) A "ruler", the Antichrist, makes a 7 year agreement which, it would seem, protects the right of Israel to conduct Levitical sacrificial worship at the temple in Jerusalem.

- (Rev. 13:1) Man of lawlessness/the beast/the Antichrist is revealed.

- (Rev. 13:1) Beast/Antichrist has 7 heads and 10 horns.

- (Rev. 13:2) Satan empowers the Antichrist.

➢ (Rev. 6:1) *Jesus breaks the first seal*

➢ (Rev. 6:2) The Antichrist has authority and conquers with the threat of war.

➢ (Rev. 6:3) *Jesus breaks the second seal*

➢ (Rev. 6:4) There is "war and slaughter everywhere".

➢ (Rev. 6:4) *Jesus breaks the third seal*

➢ (Rev. 6:6) Famine ensues such that a day's wage just pays for your

➢ meals. But the rich and powerful continue to live well.

➢ (Rev. 6:7) *Jesus breaks the forth seal*

➢ (Rev. 6:8) Wars, famine, and disease consume ¼ of the world.

➢ (Rev. 6:9) *Jesus breaks the fifth seal*

➢ (Rev. 6:9-11) More Christians are yet to be martyred.

- (Rev. 13:3) Antichrist recovers from the fatal head wound. See also verses 12 and 14.

- (Dan. 9:27) After half of this 7 year agreement, the Antichrist breaks this agreement by stopping the Levitical worship at the temple.

- **(Matt. 24:21) The Great Tribulation begins.**

- (Dan. 12:11) From the time the Antichrist halts the Levitical worship there will be 1,290 days; or 3 ½ years plus 30 days.

- (Rev. 13:4) People worship Satan who empowered the Antichrist.

- (Rev. 13:4) People worship the Antichrist.

- (Rev. 13:5) Antichrist can do whatever he wants for 3 ½ years.

- (Rev. 13:5) Antichrist blasphemes God.

- (Rev. 13:7) Antichrist wages war on Christians and overcomes them.

- (Rev. 13:11) Antichrist is joined by "another beast"; aka "the false prophet".

- (Rev. 13:12) False prophet is given all the authority of the Antichrist.

- (Rev. 13:12) False prophet requires people to worship the Antichrist.

- (Rev. 13:13) False prophet performs miracles.

- (Rev. 13:14) With miracles he deceives many, the world over.

- (2nd Thes 2:4) The Antichrist sits down in "the temple of God" proclaiming that he is God.

- (2nd Thes 2:9) Satan empowers the Antichrist to perform signs and miracles.

- (Dan. 9:27) The Antichrist sets up a sacrilegious object that desecrates the temple. It remains until his demise.

- (Matt. 24:15) The abomination of desolation stands in the holy place.

- (Matt. 24:15) Gospel preached in all the world. Then "after that" the end will come.

- (Matt. 24:21) The events occurring during this period are worse than anything that has ever happened or ever will again.

- (Rev. 13:14) False prophet has a statue of the Antichrist made.

- (Rev. 13:15) False prophet "gives life to the statue" which speaks.

- (Rev. 13:15) The statue commands that anyone refusing to worship it be executed.

- (Rev. 13:16) All who will not receive "the mark" of the Antichrist are executed.

- (Rev. 13:17) Only those with the mark of the Antichrist on their forehead or right side can buy or sell.

- (Matt. 24:24) False Christs & false prophets show great signs & wonders.

- (2nd Thes 2:11) God enables those who believe the Antichrist to sink deep into their delusions.

- **(Matt. 24:29) The Great Tribulation ends.**

- (Matt. 24:29) "Immediately after" The Tribulation, the sun will be darkened, the moon will give no light, the stars will fall from the sky, and the powers in the heavens will be shaken.

- (Rev. 6:12) *Jesus breaks the sixth seal*

- (Rev. 6:12) There is a great earthquake.

- (Rev. 6:12) The sun becomes dark as black cloth.

- ➤ (Rev. 6:12) The moon becomes blood red.

- ➤ (Rev. 6:13) Asters (glowing objects) fall from the sky.

- ➤ (Rev. 6:14) The sky rolls up like a scroll.

- ➤ (Rev. 6:14) Islands and mountains are moved.

- ➤ (Rev. 6:15) People everywhere hide.

- ➤ (Rev. 6:9) People everywhere ask for death.

- ➤ (Rev. 6:16-17) People say they are experiencing the wrath of Christ and of God the Father.

- (Matt. 24:30) "Then" the sign of Jesus' return appears in the sky.

- (Matt. 24:30) The unbelievers on earth will mourn and see Jesus returning with power and great glory.

- (Matt. 24:31) There will be a great trumpet blast.

- (Matt. 24:31) His angels gather all the believers from everywhere; earth and heaven.

- (Dan. 9:27) The fate decreed for the Antichrist is poured out on him.

- (2nd Thes 2:11) Upon His return, Jesus kills the Antichrist.

If, upon reviewing this list of events, you are convinced that you are living during The Tribulation or The Great Tribulation then go to the Verification Checklist in Chapter 13 and check the appropriate entries.

There is a division between Rev. 6:11 & 6:12. Rev. 6:1-11 speak of travesties which occur over a period of time. Verse 8 speaks of wars consuming ¼ of the world. Rev. 6:1-8 could have been placed a bit earlier on the timeline; between 2nd Thess. 2:3 and 2:7, rather than immediately after Rev. 13:2. Never-the-less Rev. 6:12-17 speak of the return of Christ to engage His enemies. Hence, these verses mark the end of The Great Tribulation. Matt. 24:29 says that after The Great Tribulation the events of Matt. 24:30-31 will occur. These events correlate directly to those of Rev. 6:12-17. At this point people recognize that they are experiencing the wrath of God. Many events occur after the 7th Seal is broken. These events are not presented in this timeline because the events presented so far are sufficient for you to determine if you are, in fact, living in The Tribulation. For information on the events occurring between the return of Christ and the death of the Antichrist, refer to our web site.

12

Composite Tribulation Timeline

- (Matt. 24:2) Destruction of the temple in Jerusalem.

- (Matt. 24:5) Many will come claiming to be "the Christ" and deceiving many.

- (Matt 24:6) Hear of wars and rumors of wars but end is not yet.

- (Matt 24:7) Nation rises against nation and kingdom against kingdom.

- (Matt. 24:7) Famines, plagues, and earthquakes around the world.

- (Matt 24:8) Jesus refers to the events of verses 5-7 as birth pangs.

- (Matt. 24:9) Christians persecuted and martyred.

- (Matt. 24:10) Many Christians lose their faith in Christ due to persecution.

- (Matt. 24:11) Many false prophets will rise up and deceive many.

- (Matt. 24:12) Love will wax cold for many.

- **The Tribulation begins**

- (2nd Thes 2:3) The great rebellion against God occurs.

- (2nd Thes 2:7) He who or that which restrains the Antichrist is removed or is no longer blocking his way.

- (2nd Thes 2:3) The Antichrist or man of lawlessness is revealed.

(Dan. 9:2,) A ruler, the Antichrist, makes a 7 year agreement which, it would seem, protects the right of Israel to conduct Levitical sacrificial worship at the temple in Jerusalem.

- (Rev. 13:1) Man of lawlessness/the beast/the Antichrist is revealed.

- (Rev. 13:1) Beast/Antichrist has 7 heads and 10 horns.

- (Rev. 13:2) Satan empowers the Antichrist.

- (Rev. 6:1) *Jesus breaks the first seal*

- (Rev. 6:2) The Antichrist has authority and conquers with the threat of war.

- (Rev. 6:3) *Jesus breaks the second seal*

- (Rev. 6:4) There is "war and slaughter everywhere".

- (Rev. 6:4) *Jesus breaks the third seal*

- (Rev. 6:6) Famine ensues such that a day's wage just pays for your

- meals. But the rich and powerful continue to live well.

- (Rev. 6:7) *Jesus breaks the forth seal*

- (Rev. 6:8) Wars, famine, and disease consume ¼ of the world.

- (Rev. 6:9) *Jesus breaks the fifth seal*

- (Rev. 6:9-11) More Christians are yet to be martyred.

- (Rev. 13:3) Antichrist recovers from the fatal head wound. See also verses 12 and 14.

- (Dan. 9:27) After half of this 7 year agreement, the Antichrist breaks this agreement by stopping the Levitical worship at the temple.

- **(Matt. 24:21) The Great Tribulation begins.**

- (Dan. 12:11) From the time the Antichrist halts the Levitical worship there will be 1,290 days; or 3 ½ years plus 30 days.

- (Rev. 13:4) People worship Satan who empowered the Antichrist.

- (Rev. 13:4) People worship the Antichrist.

- (Rev. 13:5) Antichrist can do whatever he wants for 3 ½ years.

- (Rev. 13:5) Antichrist blasphemes God.

- (Rev. 13:7) Antichrist wages war on Christians and overcomes them.

- (Rev. 13:11) Antichrist is joined by "another beast"; aka "the false prophet".

- (Rev. 13:12) False prophet is given all the authority of the Antichrist.

- (Rev. 13:12) False prophet requires people to worship the Antichrist.

- (Rev. 13:13) False prophet performs miracles.

- (Rev. 13:14) With miracles he deceives many, the world over.

- (2ⁿᵈ Thes 2:4) The Antichrist sits down in "the temple of God" proclaiming that he is God.

- (2ⁿᵈ Thes 2:9) Satan empowers the Antichrist to perform signs and miracles.

- (Dan. 9:27) The Antichrist sets up a sacrilegious object that desecrates the temple. It remains until his demise.

- (Matt. 24:15) The abomination of desolation stands in the holy place.

- (Matt. 24:15) Gospel preached in all the world. Then <u>"after that" the end will come.</u>

- (Matt. 24:21) The events occurring during this period are worse than anything that has ever happened or ever will again.

- (Rev. 13:14) False prophet has a statue of the Antichrist made.

- (Rev. 13:15) False prophet "gives life to the statue" which speaks.

- (Rev. 13:15) The statue commands that anyone refusing to worship it be executed.

- (Rev. 13:16) All who will not receive "the mark" of the Antichrist are executed.

- (Rev. 13:17) Only those with the mark of the Antichrist on their forehead or right side can buy or sell.

- (Matt. 24:24) False Christs & false prophets show great signs & wonders.

- (2ⁿᵈ Thes 2:11) God enables those who believe the Antichrist to sink deep into their delusions.

- **(Matt. 24:29) The Great Tribulation ends.**

- (Matt. 24:29) "Immediately after" The Tribulation, the sun will be darkened, the moon will give no light, the stars will fall from the sky, and the powers in the heavens will be shaken.

- (Rev. 6:12) *Jesus breaks the sixth seal*

- (Rev. 6:12) There is a great earthquake.

- (Rev. 6:12) The sun becomes dark as black cloth.

- (Rev. 6:12) The moon becomes blood red.

- (Rev. 6:13) Asters (glowing objects) fall from the sky.

- (Rev. 6:14) The sky rolls up like a scroll.

- (Rev. 6:14) Islands and mountains are moved.

- (Rev. 6:15) People everywhere hide.

- (Rev. 6:9) People everywhere ask for death.

- (Rev. 6:16-17) People say they are experiencing the wrath of Christ and of God the Father.

- (Matt. 24:30) "Then" the sign of Jesus' return appears in the sky.

- (Matt. 24:30) The unbelievers on earth will mourn and see Jesus returning with power and great glory.

- (Matt. 24:31) There will be a great trumpet blast.

- (Matt. 24:31) His angels gather all the believers from everywhere; earth and heaven.

- (Dan. 9:27) The fate decreed for the Antichrist is poured out on him.

- (2nd Thes 2:11) Upon His return, Jesus kills the Antichrist.

By checking off the events on the Composite Tribulation Timeline, you can get a good idea of what still lays ahead.

If you would like to customize the timeline then go our web site where you will find a timeline spreadsheet which you can modify.

13

Verification Checklist

Christians

- ○ I'm a Christian
- ○ I'm <u>not</u> a Christian
- ○ I'm not sure

The rapture

- ○ I'm sure the rapture has occurred
- ○ I'm sure the rapture has <u>not</u> occurred
- ○ I'm not sure

The Tribulation

- ○ I'm sure The Tribulation has begun
- ○ I'm sure The Tribulation has <u>not</u> begun
- ○ I'm not sure

The Great Tribulation has begun

- ○ I'm sure The Great Tribulation has begun
- ○ I'm sure The Great Tribulation has <u>not</u> begun
- ○ I'm not sure

Now that you have finished this book, it's time to review the check list above. If, you have verified that you are in The Tribulation and you are not a Christian then it's time you became one. If you can verify that the rapture has occurred and you always thought you were a Christian then it's time to follow the steps laid out in Chapter 3 "Christian?". If you have just become a Christian then study Chapters 4 and 5 on being Combat Ready and on exercising Kingdom Authority.

If you checked "I'm not sure" on any of the above then go to www.FromHereToEternity.info and dig deeper until you are sure.

Regardless, we encourage you to go there to deepen your understanding so that you can help others.

Web Site Registration

Please go to www.FromHereToEternity.info and register so that you can access the valuable information we have compiled for you.

But, Beware! The further into The Tribulation you are the greater is the likelihood that our web site has been compromised by agents of the Antichrist.

Remember though, the Bible is your sure and final guide. Read it and pray for understanding!

May God be with you.

May He bless you and keep you.

May we all meet when Jesus reigns from Jerusalem!

ABOUT THE AUTHOR

Reverend William G. Woltman (aka WillieG) is the Senior Pastor of the Heartland Vineyard Church in Avon Park, Florida. He did his graduate work in Biblical Studies at the Reformed Theological Seminary in Charlotte, NC and his undergraduate work in Philosophy at the University of Houston.

See: www.HeartlandVineyardChurch.com